MW01382888

GARDEN OF PRAYER
JOURNAL

GARDEN OF PRAYER
JOURNAL

GARDEN OF PRAYER
JOURNAL

The Beautiful Garden of Prayer

There's a garden where Jesus is waiting,
There's a place that is wondrously fair,
For it glows with the light of His presence.
'Tis the beautiful garden of prayer.

Oh, the beautiful garden, the garden of prayer!
Oh, the beautiful garden of prayer!
There my Savior awaits, and He opens the gates
To the beautiful garden of prayer.

There's a garden where Jesus is waiting,
And I go with my burden and care,
Just to learn from His lips words of comfort
In the beautiful garden of prayer.

There's a garden where Jesus is waiting,
And He bids you to come, meet Him there;
Just to bow and receive a new blessing
In the beautiful garden of prayer.

—Eleanor Allen Schroll

_____

_____

_____

_____

_____

_____

_____

_____

_____

_____

_____

_____

_____

_____

The Christian life is not a constant high. I have my moments of deep discouragement. I have to go to God in prayer with tears in my eyes, and say, "O God, forgive me," or "Help me."

—Billy Graham

ASK, AND IT WILL BE GIVEN TO YOU; SEEK, AND YOU WILL FIND; KNOCK, AND IT WILL BE OPENED TO YOU. FOR EVERYONE WHO ASKS RECEIVES, AND HE WHO SEEKS FINDS, AND TO HIM WHO KNOCKS IT WILL BE OPENED.

—Matthew 7:7-8

Prayer is no fitful, short-lived thing. It is no voice crying unheard and unheeded in the silence. It is a voice which goes into God's ear, and it lives as long as God's ear is open to holy pleas, as long as God's heart is alive to holy things. God shapes the world by prayer.

—*E. M. Bounds*

HEAR MY PRAYER, O GOD; GIVE EAR TO THE WORDS OF MY MOUTH.

—Psalm 54:2 KJV

The purpose of all prayer is to find God's will

and to make that will our prayer.

—Catherine Marshall

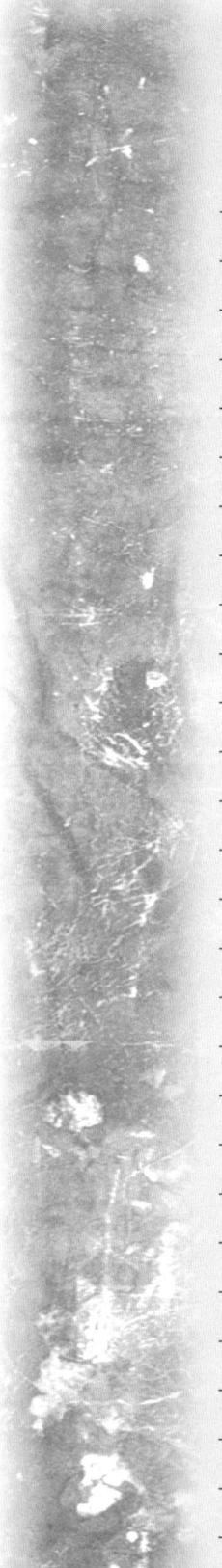

TAKE YE HEED, WATCH AND PRAY:
FOR YE KNOW NOT WHEN THE TIME IS.

—Mark 13:33 KJV

Prayer is not so much an act as it is an attitude
—an attitude of dependency, dependency upon God.
—Arthur W. Pink

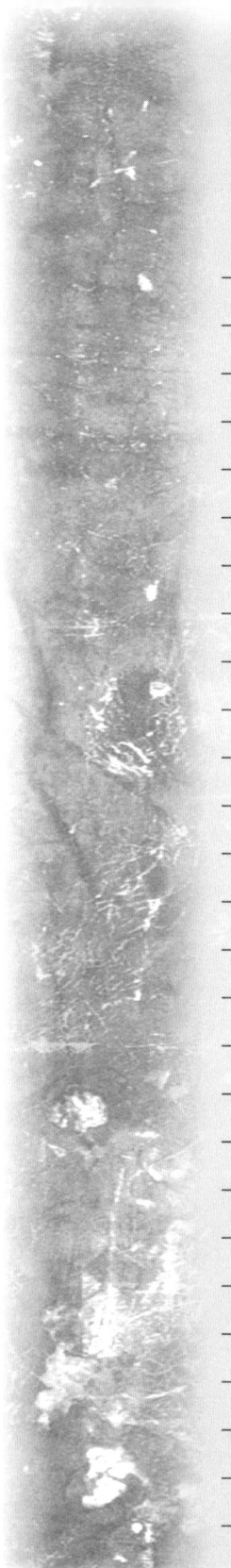

NOW, O MY GOD, I PRAY, LET YOUR EYES BE OPEN AND YOUR EARS ATTENTIVE TO THE PRAYER OFFERED IN THIS PLACE.

—2 Chronicles 6:40 NASV

To pray is nothing more involved than to open the door, giving Jesus access to our needs and permitting Him to exercise His own power in dealing with them.

—*O. Hallesby*

"For I know the plans I have for you," declares the LORD, "plans to prosper you and not to harm you, plans to give you hope and a future. Then you will call upon me and come and pray to me, and I will listen to you. You will seek me and find me when you seek me with all your heart."

—Jeremiah 29:11-13 NIV

We forget that God sometimes has to say No. We pray to Him as our heavenly Father, and like wise human fathers, He often says, No, not from whim or caprice, but from wisdom and from love, and knowing what is best for us.

—Peter Marshall

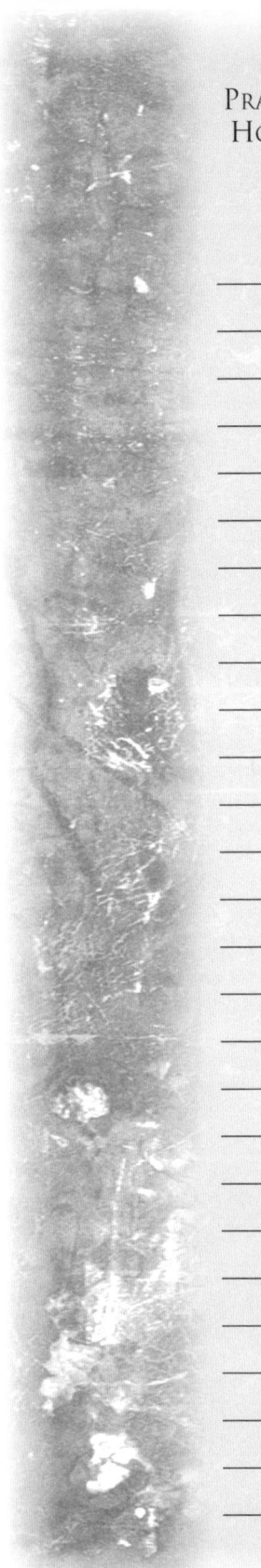

PRAY AT ALL TIMES AND ON EVERY OCCASION IN THE POWER OF THE HOLY SPIRIT. STAY ALERT AND BE PERSISTENT IN YOUR PRAYERS FOR ALL CHRISTIANS EVERYWHERE.

—Ephesians 6:18 NLT

Prayer does not cause faith to work, faith causes prayer to work.
—Gloria Copeland

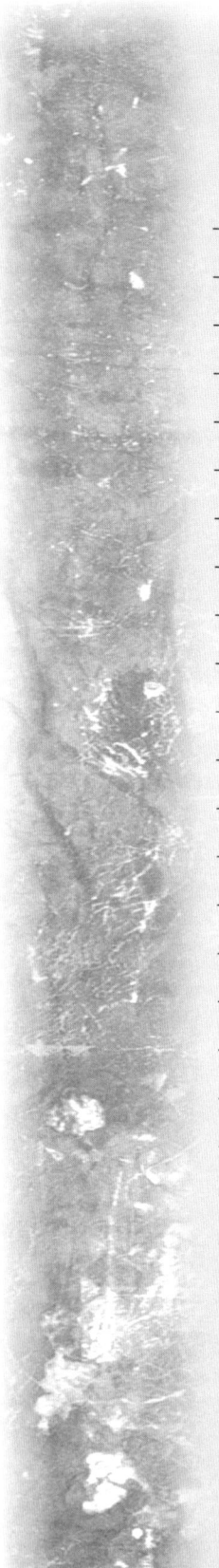

LET YOUR HOPE MAKE YOU GLAD. BE PATIENT IN TIME OF TROUBLE
AND NEVER STOP PRAYING.

—Romans 12:12 CEV

Anything big enough to occupy our minds

is big enough to hang a prayer on.

—George Macdonald

AND LOVE GOD, YOUR God, LISTENING OBEDIENTLY TO HIM, FIRM-
LY EMBRACING HIM. OH YES, HE IS LIFE ITSELF.

—*Deuteronomy 30:20 THE MESSAGE*

Someone once said that prayer is the key to the morning and the bolt to the evening. Another person wrote that a day hemmed in prayer seldom comes unraveled. There are no short-cuts: Spiritual vitality depends on a regular and rigorous habit of daily prayer.

—*Robert J. Morgan*

WHATEVER YOU ASK FOR IN PRAYER WITH FAITH, YOU WILL RECEIVE.
—*Matthew 21:22 NRSV*

How often has God said no to my earnest prayers that He might answer my deepest longings, give me something more, something better.
—Ruth Bell Graham

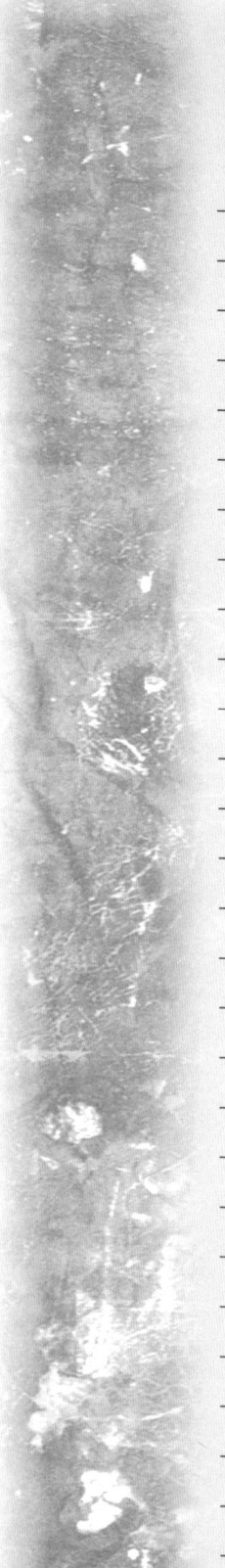

GIVE THANKS TO THE LORD, FOR HE IS GOOD,
HIS LOVE ENDURES FOREVER.

—*Psalm 107:1 NIV*

NOW THEREFORE, I PRAY, IF I HAVE FOUND GRACE IN YOUR SIGHT,
SHOW ME NOW YOUR WAY, THAT I MAY KNOW YOU AND THAT I MAY
FIND GRACE IN YOUR SIGHT.

—Exodus 33:13

Is prayer your steering wheel or your spare tire?
—Corrie ten Boom

_____
_____
_____
_____
_____
_____
_____
_____
_____
_____
_____
_____
_____
_____
_____
_____
_____
_____
_____
_____
_____
_____
_____
_____
_____

Pray all the time, and make it a habit to listen with all your heart for his voice.
—Luci Swindoll

DON'T WORRY ABOUT ANYTHING; INSTEAD, PRAY ABOUT EVERY-
THING. TELL GOD WHAT YOU NEED, AND THANK HIM
FOR ALL HE HAS DONE.

—Philippians 4:6 NLT

Allow your dreams a place in your prayers and plans. God-given dreams can help you move into the future He is preparing for you.

—*Barbara Johnson*

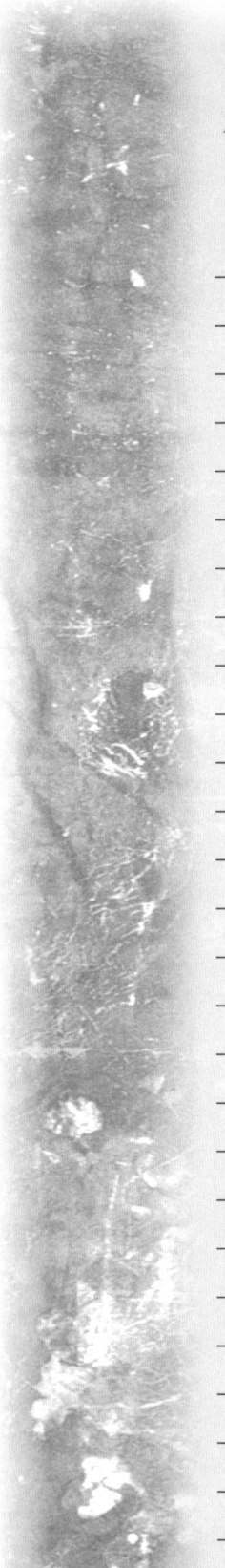

CONFESS YOUR FAULTS ONE TO ANOTHER, AND PRAY ONE FOR ANOTHER, THAT YE MAY BE HEALED. THE EFFECTUAL FERVENT PRAYER OF A RIGHTEOUS MAN AVAILETH MUCH.

—James 5:16 KJV

God puts a great deal more value on our prayers than we do. He considers prayer to be a serious thing that can influence events in this world —both events in our personal lives and events in world history and current events.

—Robert J. Morgan

_____

_____

_____

_____

_____

_____

_____

_____

_____

_____

_____

_____

_____

_____

_____

_____

_____

_____

_____

_____

_____

_____

_____

_____

_____

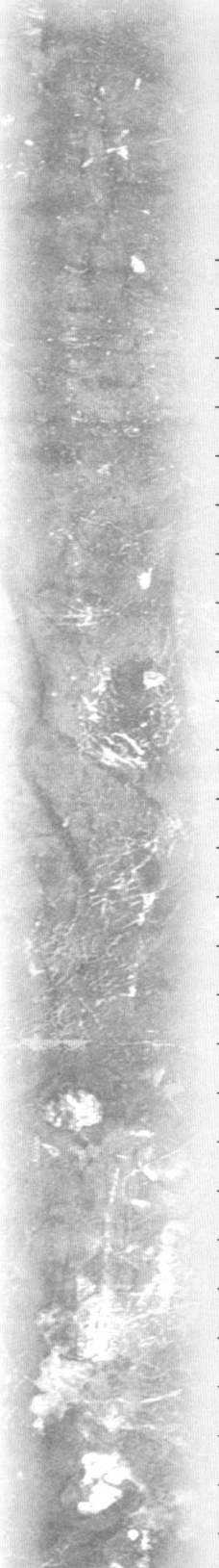

MOREOVER, AS FOR ME, FAR BE IT FROM ME THAT I SHOULD SIN AGAINST THE LORD BY CEASING TO PRAY FOR YOU, BUT I WILL INSTRUCT YOU IN THE GOOD AND RIGHT WAY.

—1 Samuel 12:23

In quiet conversations with our Lord, we hear in our longing hearts of His expansive love, which helps us to move from our inner conflict to His peaceful resolution.

—Patsy Clairmont

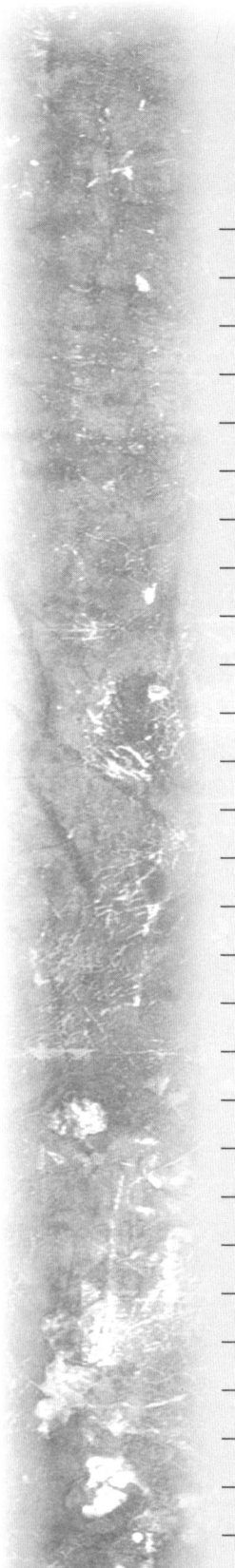

CAST YOUR CARES ON THE LORD AND HE WILL SUSTAIN YOU.

—Psalm 55:22 NIV

Prayer is not a matter of getting what we want the most. Prayer is a matter of giving ourselves to God and learning His laws, so that He can do through us what He wants the most.

—*Agnes Sanford*

CALL TO ME AND I WILL ANSWER YOU AND TELL YOU GREAT AND
UNSEARCHABLE THINGS YOU DO NOT KNOW.

—Jeremiah 33:3

When you are in the dark, listen,
and God will give you a very precious message.
—Oswald Chambers

HEAR MY CRY, O GOD; ATTEND TO MY PRAYER.

—Psalm 61:1

_____

_____

_____

_____

_____

_____

_____

_____

_____

_____

_____

_____

_____

_____

_____

_____

_____

_____

_____

_____

_____

_____

_____

_____

_____

_____

We must focus on prayer as the main thrust to accomplish God's will and purpose on earth. The forces against us have never been greater and this is the only way we can release God's power to become victorious.

—John Maxwell

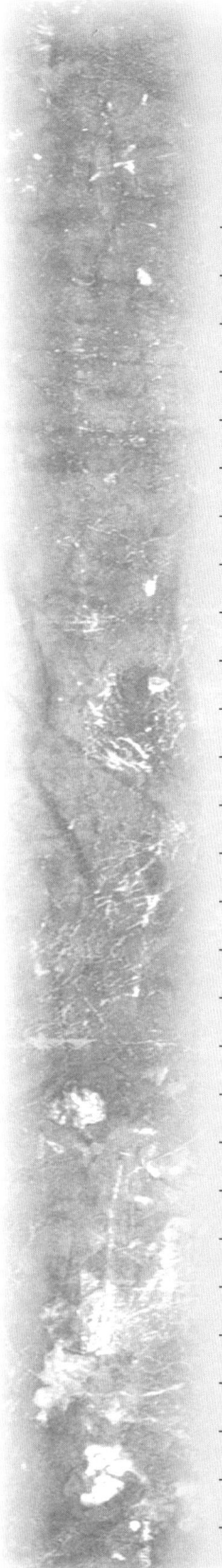

THEIR VOICE WAS HEARD AND THEIR PRAYER CAME TO HIS HOLY
DWELLING PLACE, TO HEAVEN.

—*2 Chronicles 30:27 NASB*

Through prayer, God greatly multiplies our efforts. What we can do on our own is limited, but what God can do is endless.

—*John Maxwell*

HE WAS TELLING THEM A PARABLE TO SHOW THAT AT ALL TIMES THEY
OUGHT TO PRAY AND NOT TO LOSE HEART.

—Luke 18:1 NASV

*To get nations back on their feet,
we must first get down on our knees.*
—Billy Graham

While Jesus lived on earth, he prayed to God and asked God for help. He prayed with loud cries and tears to the One who could save him from death, and his prayer was heard because he trusted God.

—Hebrews 5:7 NCV

Perhaps one reason God delays His answers to our prayers is because He knows we need to be with Him far more than we need the things we ask of Him.

—Ben Patterson

HANNAH PRAYED: YOU MAKE ME STRONG AND HAPPY, LORD. YOU RESCUED ME. NOW I CAN BE GLAD AND LAUGH AT MY ENEMIES.

—1 Samuel 2:1 CEV

No matter what has happened to you or is happening in the world around you, God promises to protect you as you walk with Him. Pray that He will and trust Him to do so.

—Stormie Omartian

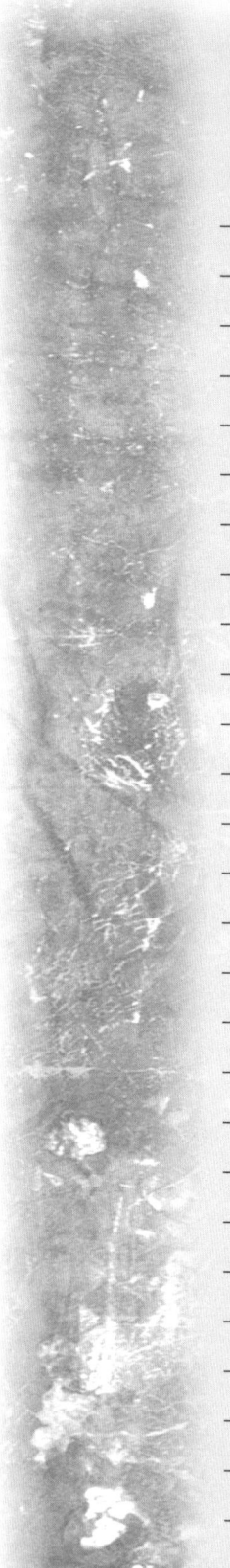

PLEASE ANSWER MY PRAYER AND THE PRAYER OF YOUR OTHER
SERVANTS WHO GLADLY HONOR YOUR NAME.

—Nehemiah 1:11 CEV

Ask God to fit you with His armor when you pray. Trust the Lord to guard your time with him. If you fail, don't be depressed. God still waits for you. The victory in the battle of prayer is yours.

—*Charles Stanley*

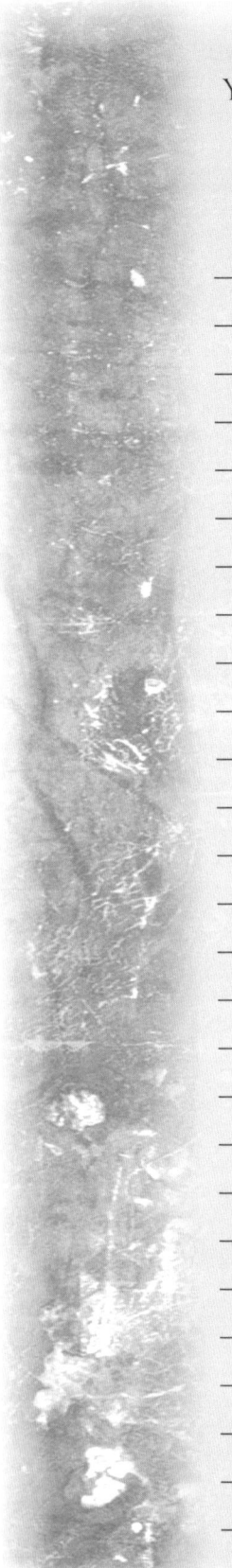

YET REGARD THE PRAYER OF YOUR SERVANT AND HIS SUPPLICATION,
O LORD MY GOD, AND LISTEN TO THE CRY AND THE PRAYER
WHICH YOUR SERVANT IS PRAYING BEFORE YOU TODAY.

—1 Kings 8:28

When you pray, ask God to reveal His will for your life and the situation you are facing. Don't just get caught up in praying for material gain. God provides where there is a need. His greatest desire is for you to learn to trust him in prayer.

—*Charles Stanley*

BE SURE TO OBEY ALL MY INSTRUCTIONS. AND REMEMBER, NEVER PRAY TO OR SWEAR BY ANY OTHER GODS. DO NOT EVEN MENTION THEIR NAMES.

—*Exodus 23:13 NLT*

When you pray for anyone you tend to modify your personal attitude toward him.

—Norman Vincent Peale

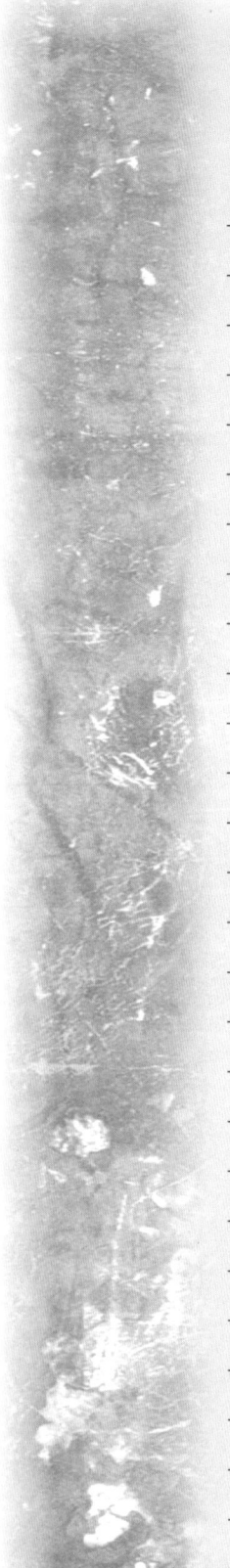

I SOUGHT THE LORD, AND HE HEARD ME, AND DELIVERED ME FROM ALL MY FEARS.

—*Psalm 34:4*

I've decided to change the way I pray. I used to pray with a whole long list of things I wanted God to do; now I pray for wisdom, and I pray to be more like Christ.

—Sheila Walsh

AND THEY CONTINUED STEADFASTLY IN THE APOSTLES' DOCTRINE
AND FELLOWSHIP, AND IN THE BREAKING OF BREAD, AND IN PRAYERS.

—*Acts 2:42*

God can change our circumstances, but sometimes He waits for us to show real desire for change as well as our faith in Him.

—Anne Graham Lotz

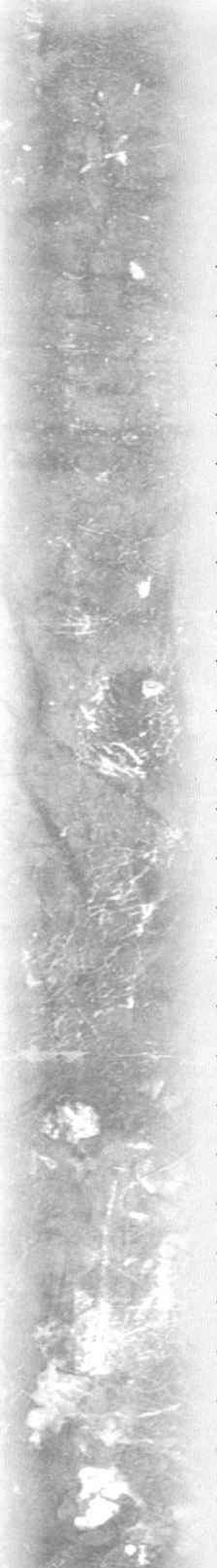

THE LORD RESTORED JOB'S LOSSES WHEN HE PRAYED FOR HIS
FRIENDS. INDEED THE LORD GAVE JOB TWICE AS MUCH
AS HE HAD BEFORE.

—Job 42:10

Our prayers may be awkward. Our attempts may be feeble. But since the power of prayer is in the one who hears it and not in the one who says it, our prayers do make a difference.

—*Max Lucado*

HE HEEDED THEIR PRAYER, BECAUSE THEY PUT THEIR TRUST IN HIM.

—1 Chronicles 5:20

Our responsibility is to keep knocking at God's door . . . to keep believing God will answer our prayers. . . . Patiently but expectantly wait on the Lord.

—Thelma Wells

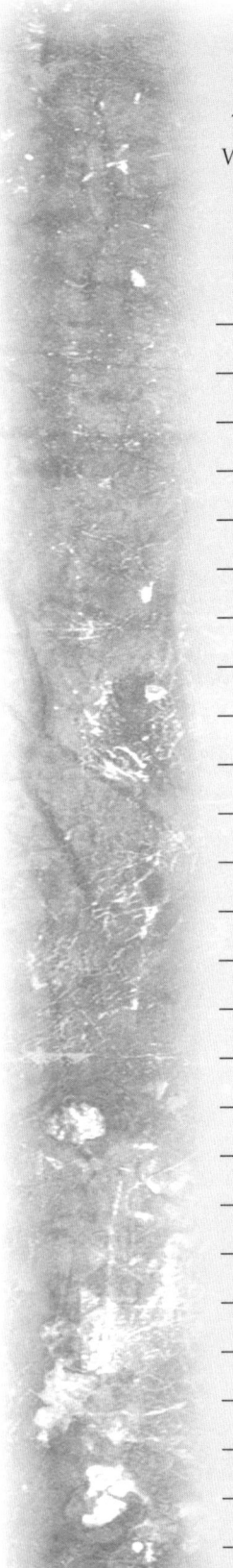

IF MY PEOPLE WHO ARE CALLED BY MY NAME WILL HUMBLE
THEMSELVES, AND PRAY AND SEEK MY FACE, AND TURN FROM THEIR
WICKED WAYS, THEN I WILL HEAR FROM HEAVEN, AND WILL FORGIVE
THEIR SIN AND HEAL THEIR LAND.

—2 Chronicles 7:14

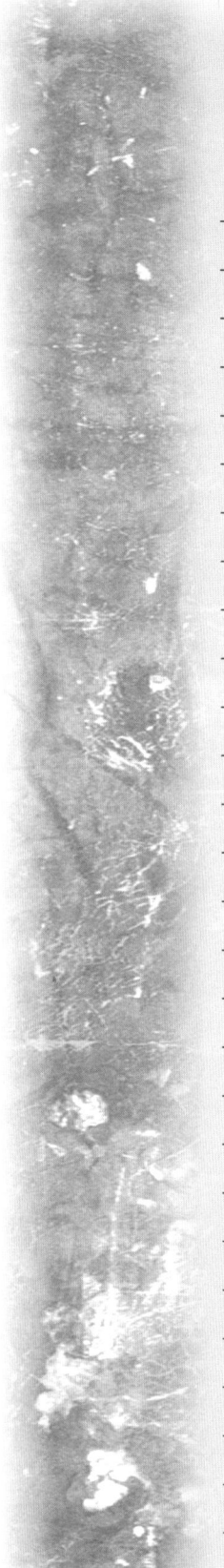

I DO NOT PRAY FOR THESE ALONE, BUT ALSO FOR THOSE WHO WILL BELIEVE IN ME THROUGH THEIR WORD.

—John 17:20

WHEN I PRAY, YOU ANSWER ME; YOU ENCOURAGE ME BY GIVING ME
THE STRENGTH I NEED.

—Psalm 138:3 NLT

I got up early this morning,
And paused before entering the day,
I had so much to accomplish—
I had to take time to pray.
— Grace L. Naessens

GOD HAS SEEN HOW I NEVER STOP PRAYING FOR YOU,
WHILE I SERVE HIM WITH ALL MY HEART AND TELL
THE GOOD NEWS ABOUT HIS SON.

—*Romans 1:9 CEV*

Prayer is the place of refuge for every worry, a foundation for cheerfulness, a source of constant happiness, a protection against sadness.

—St. John Chrysostom

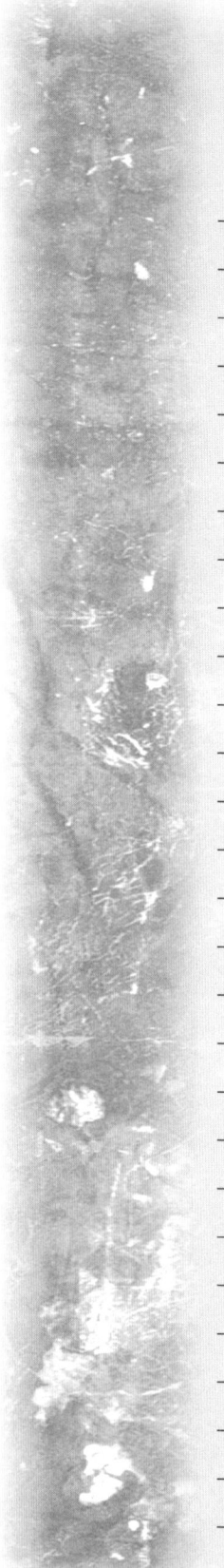

YOU WILL MAKE YOUR PRAYER TO HIM, HE WILL HEAR YOU, AND YOU WILL PAY YOUR VOWS.

—Job 22:27

Prayer is not monologue, but dialogue; God's voice is its most essential part. Listening to God's voice is the secret of the assurance that He will listen to mine.

—Andrew Murray

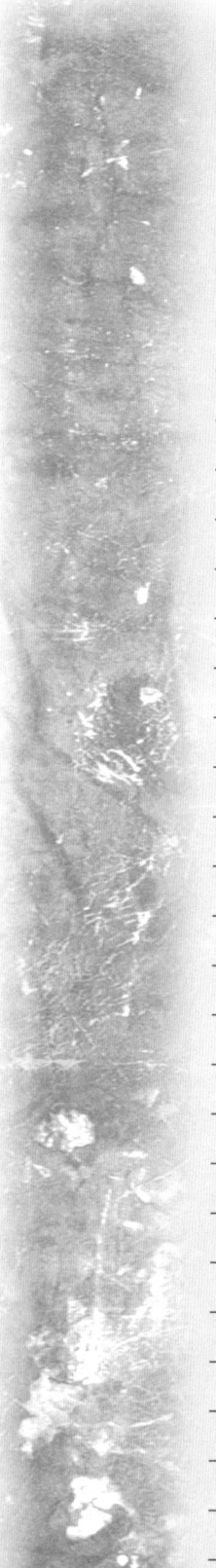

HE SHALL PRAY TO GOD, AND HE WILL DELIGHT IN HIM,
HE SHALL SEE HIS FACE WITH JOY, FOR HE RESTORES TO MAN
HIS RIGHTEOUSNESS.

—Job 33:26

Prayer is a choice. For us to pray to give thanks, or to voice our questions and doubts shows that we are choosing to leave an opening in our spirits. Without this opening, there is no vessel, no place into which God can breathe.

—Joanna Laufer

GIVE EAR TO MY WORDS, O LORD, CONSIDER MY MEDITATION. HEARKEN UNTO THE VOICE OF MY CRY, MY KING, AND MY GOD: FOR UNTO THEE WILL I PRAY. MY VOICE SHALT THOU HEAR IN THE MORNING, O LORD; IN THE MORNING WILL I DIRECT MY PRAYER UNTO THEE, AND WILL LOOK UP.

—Psalm 5:1-3 KJV

Begin by thanking Him for some little thing, and then go on, day by day, adding to your subjects of praise; thus you will find their numbers grow wonderfully; and, in the same proportion, will your subjects of murmuring and complaining diminish, until you see in everything some cause for thanksgiving.

—*Priscilla Maurice*

Faith in a prayer-hearing God will make
a prayer-loving Christian.
—Andrew Murray

HEAR A JUST CAUSE, O LORD, ATTEND TO MY CRY; GIVE EAR TO MY
PRAYER WHICH IS NOT FROM DECEITFUL LIPS.

—Psalm 17:1

Lift up your eyes. The heavenly Father waits to bless you ~in inconceivable ways to make your life what you never dreamed it could be.

—Anne Ortlund

YET THE LORD WILL COMMAND HIS LOVINGKINDNESS IN THE DAY TIME; AND IN THE NIGHT HIS SONG SHALL BE WITH ME, AND MY PRAYER UNTO THE GOD OF MY LIFE.

—Psalm 42:8 KJV

Lord, make my life a window for Your light to shine through and a mirror to reflect Your love to all I meet. Amen.

—*Robert Schuller*

LET US THEN APPROACH THE THRONE OF GRACE WITH CONFIDENCE,
SO THAT WE MAY RECEIVE MERCY AND FIND GRACE TO HELP US IN
OUR TIME OF NEED.

—Hebrews 4:16 NIV

Prayer has mighty power to move mountains because the Holy Spirit is ready both to encourage our praying and to remove the mountains hindering us. Prayer has the power to change mountains into highways.

—Wesley L. Duewel

BUT CERTAINLY GOD HAS HEARD ME; HE HAS ATTENDED TO THE VOICE OF MY PRAYER.

—*Psalm 66:19*

I have benefited by my praying for others; for by making an errand to God for them, I have gotten something for myself.

—*Samuel Rutherford*

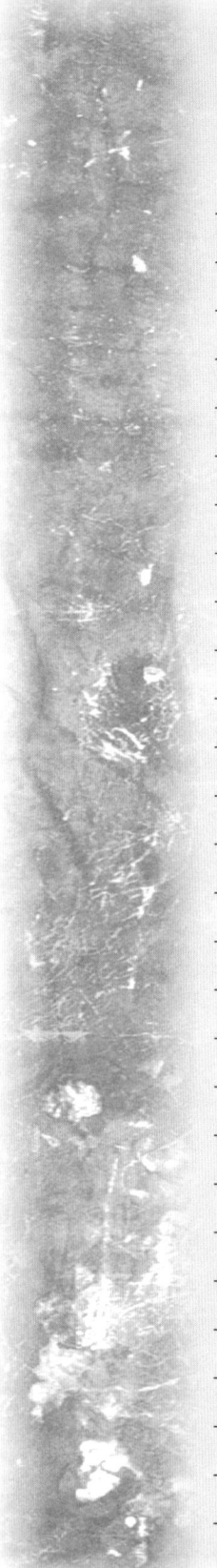

EVENING AND MORNING AND AT NOON I WILL PRAY, AND CRY ALOUD, AND HE SHALL HEAR MY VOICE.

—Psalm 55:17 KJV

We pray for the big things and forget to give thanks for the ordinary, small (and yet not so small) gifts. How can God entrust great things to one who will not thankfully receive from Him the little things?

—*Dietrich Bonhoeffer*

He shall regard the prayer of the destitute, And shall not despise their prayer.

—*Psalm 102:17 NRSV*

If you can't pray like you want to, pray as you can.
God knows what you mean.
—Vance Havner

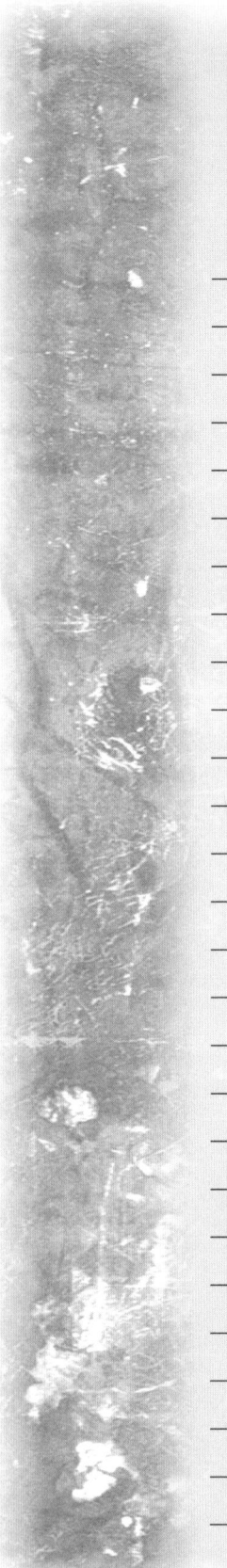

FOR THE EYES OF THE LORD ARE ON THE RIGHTEOUS, AND HIS
EARS ARE OPEN TO THEIR PRAYERS; BUT THE FACE OF THE LORD IS
AGAINST THOSE WHO DO EVIL.

—1 Peter 3:12

God expects to hear from you, before you can expect to hear from Him.
—William Gurnall

CONTINUE TO PRAY AS YOU ARE DIRECTED BY THE HOLY SPIRIT.

—Jude 1:20 NLT

I have been driven many times to my knees by the overwhelming conviction that I had nowhere else to go.

—*Abraham Lincoln*

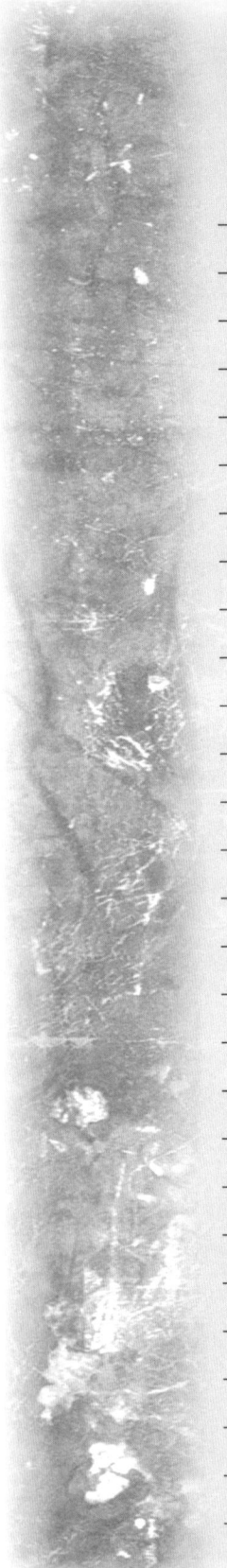

LISTEN TO MY CRY FOR HELP, MY KING AND MY GOD,
FOR TO YOU I PRAY.

—*Psalm 5:2 NIV*

The best way to get what you pray for is to pray for things for other people. To get things for ourselves, well, that is why God invented work.
—*Otto Biel*

EACH EXCLAMATION IS A TRIGGER TO PRAYER. I FIND MYSELF PRAYING
FOR YOU WITH A GLAD HEART.

—*Philippians 1:4 THE MESSAGE*

Prayer does not equip us for the greater work . . .

prayer is the greater work.
—Oswald Chambers

Therefore we also pray always for you that our God would count you worthy of this calling, and fulfill all the good pleasure of His goodness and the work of faith with power.

—*2 Thessalonians 1:11*

Prayer is more like listening than anything else—being quiet in God's presence, waiting on God until we know what to do.

—*David Roper*

HEAR MY PRAYER, O LORD! AND LET MY CRY FOR HELP COME TO YOU.

— Psalm 102:1 NASV

We must not sit still and look for miracles; up and doing, and the Lord will be with thee. Prayer and pains, through faith in Christ Jesus, will do anything.

—*Sir John Elliott*

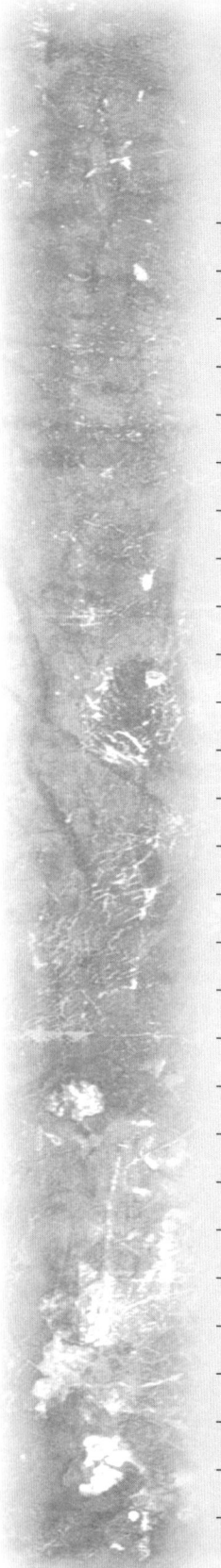

THE LORD IS FAR FROM THE WICKED, BUT HE HEARS THE PRAYER OF THE RIGHTEOUS.

—*Proverbs 15:29*

Prayer lays hold of God's plan and becomes the link between His will and its accomplishment on earth. Amazing things happen, and we are given the privilege of being the channels of the Holy Spirit's prayer.

—Elisabeth Elliot

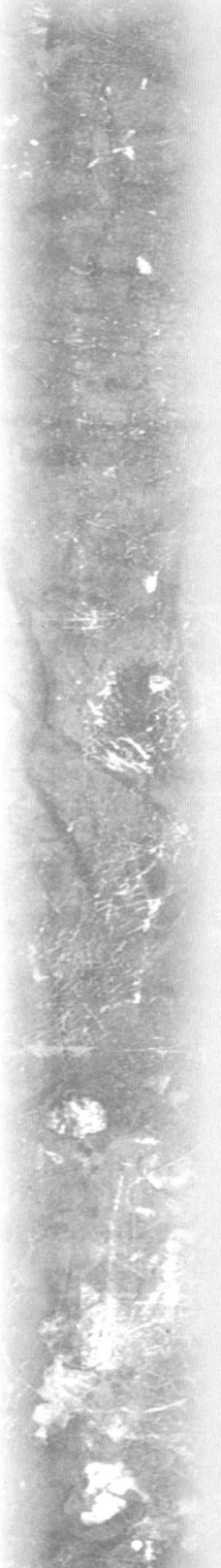

I CALL ON YOU, O GOD, FOR YOU WILL ANSWER ME;
GIVE EAR TO ME AND HEAR MY PRAYER.

—*Psalm 17:6 NIV*

Never let your head hang down. Never give up and sit down and grieve. Find another way. And don't pray when it rains if you don't pray when the sun shines.

—Leroy "Satchel" Paige

I WILL PRAY WITH THE SPIRIT, AND I WILL ALSO PRAY WITH THE UNDERSTANDING. I WILL SING WITH THE SPIRIT, AND I WILL ALSO SING WITH THE UNDERSTANDING.

—1 Corinthians 14:15

Jesus commands us to 'watch and pray.' If we are able to be persons of faith, then we will be persons of prayer. If we are to be persons of hope and healing in the world, then we will be persons for whom living is praying, and praying is living. In short, we have no choice but to pray.

—*Conrad Hoover*

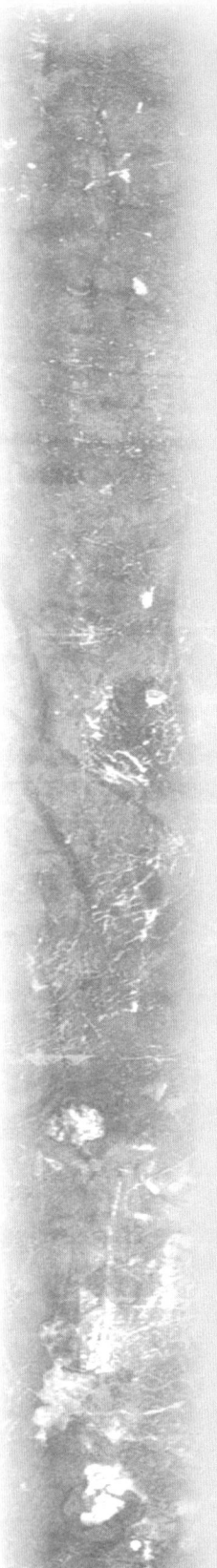

LISTEN TO MY PRAYER, O GOD, DO NOT IGNORE MY PLEA.

—Psalm 55:1 NIV

The joy and pleasure of speaking with the Lord is far superior to anything life on this earth affords. Through prayer I become centered and serene. When it's quiet and still, I sense the Lord comes near as I enter his presence.

—*Luci Swindoll*

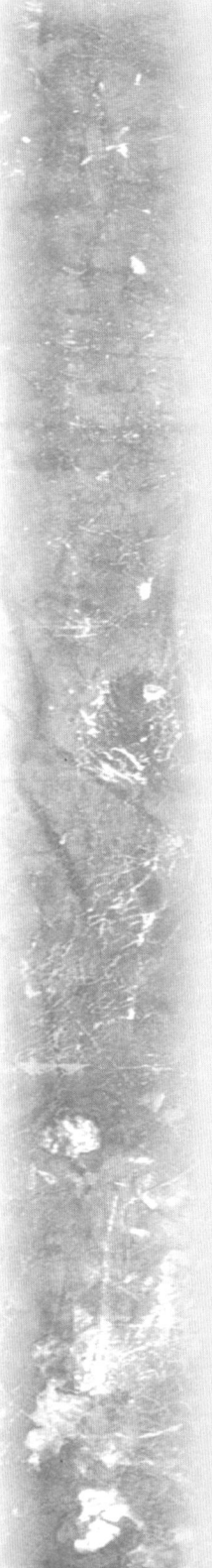

BLESSED BE GOD, WHO HAS NOT TURNED AWAY MY PRAYER,
NOR HIS MERCY FROM ME!

—Psalm 66:20

We must alter our lives in order to alter our hearts, for it is impossible to live one way and pray another.
—William Law

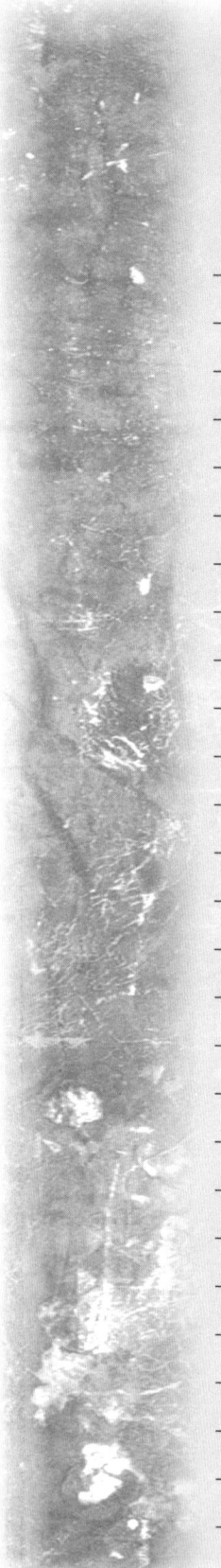

PLEASE HELP US BY PRAYING FOR US. THEN MANY PEOPLE WILL GIVE
THANKS FOR THE BLESSINGS WE RECEIVE IN ANSWER
TO ALL THESE PRAYERS.

—2 Corinthians 1:11 CEV

God warms his hands at man's heart when he prays.
—*John Masefield*

WHEN MY SOUL FAINTED WITHIN ME I REMEMBERED THE LORD:
AND MY PRAYER CAME IN UNTO THEE, INTO THINE HOLY TEMPLE.

—Jonah 2:7 KJV

The more praying there is in the world, the better the world will be, the mightier the forces against evil everywhere.

—E. M. Bounds

BUT I SAY TO YOU, LOVE YOUR ENEMIES, BLESS THOSE WHO CURSE YOU, DO GOOD TO THOSE WHO HATE YOU, AND PRAY FOR THOSE WHO SPITEFULLY USE YOU AND PERSECUTE YOU, THAT YOU MAY BE SONS OF YOUR FATHER IN HEAVEN; FOR HE MAKES HIS SUN RISE ON THE EVIL AND ON THE GOOD, AND SENDS RAIN ON THE JUST AND ON THE UNJUST.

—Matthew 5:44-45

Prayer teaches trust in God through waiting upon His timing.
—Becky Tirabassi

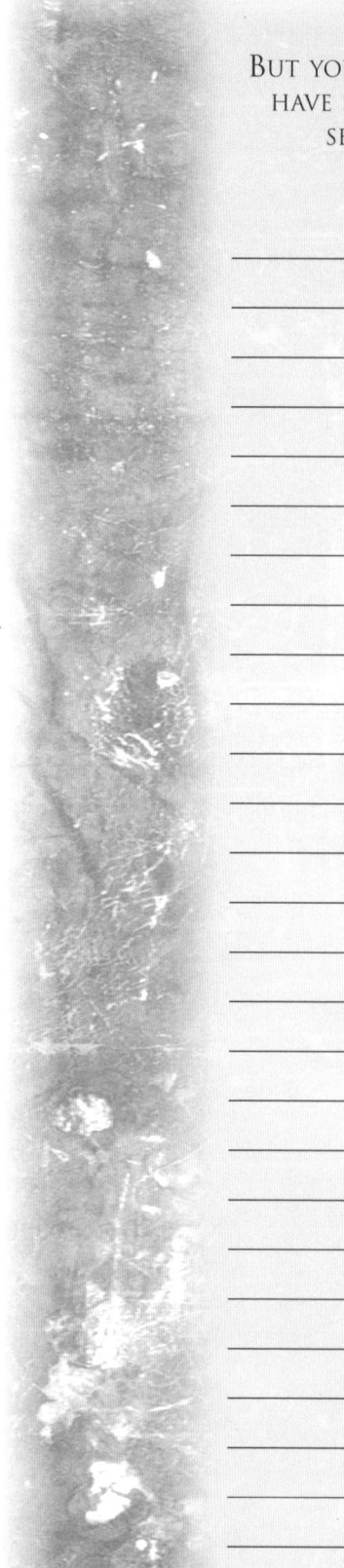

BUT YOU, WHEN YOU PRAY, GO INTO YOUR ROOM, AND WHEN YOU
HAVE SHUT YOUR DOOR, PRAY TO YOUR FATHER WHO IS IN THE
SECRET PLACE; AND YOUR FATHER WHO SEES IN SECRET
WILL REWARD YOU OPENLY.

—Matthew 6:6

Prayer is not merely an occasional impulse to which we respond when we are in trouble: prayer is a life attitude.

— Walter A. Mueller

THE END OF ALL THINGS IS NEAR. THEREFORE BE CLEAR MINDED AND SELF-CONTROLLED SO THAT YOU CAN PRAY.

—1 Peter 4:7 NIV

Work as if you were to live a hundred years.
Pray as if you were to die tomorrow.
—Benjamin Franklin

WATCH THEREFORE, AND PRAY ALWAYS THAT YOU MAY BE COUNTED WORTHY TO ESCAPE ALL THESE THINGS THAT WILL COME TO PASS, AND TO STAND BEFORE THE SON OF MAN.

—Luke 21:36

Prayer is the place where burdens are shifted.
—Barbara Johnson

And I will pray the Father, and He will give you another Helper, that He may abide with you forever.

—John 14:16

Those who know God the best are the richest and most powerful in prayer. Little acquaintance with God, and strangeness and coldness to Him, make prayer a rare and feeble thing.

—*E. M. Bounds*

WHEN YOU PRAY, DON'T TALK ON AND ON AS PEOPLE DO WHO
DON'T KNOW GOD. THEY THINK GOD LIKES TO HEAR LONG PRAYERS.

—*Matthew 6:7 CEV*

This is our Lord's will . . . that our prayer and our trust be, alike, large. For if we do not trust as much as we pray, we fail in full worship to our Lord in our prayer; and also we hinder and hurt ourselves.

—Julian of Norwich

WHATEVER YOU ASK FOR IN PRAYER WITH FAITH, YOU WILL RECEIVE.
—*Matthew 21:22 NRSV*

God does not stand afar off as I struggle to speak. He cares enough to listen with more than casual attention. He translates my scrubby words and hears what is truly inside. He hears my sighs and uncertain gropings as fine prose.

—*Timothy Jones*

SO I TELL YOU, WHATEVER YOU ASK FOR IN PRAYER, BELIEVE THAT YOU HAVE RECEIVED IT, AND IT WILL BE YOURS.

—Mark 11:24 NRSV

Rich is the person who has a praying friend.
—Janice Hughes

BUT I HAVE PRAYED FOR YOU, THAT YOUR FAITH SHOULD NOT FAIL;
AND WHEN YOU HAVE RETURNED TO ME, STRENGTHEN YOUR
BRETHREN.

—Luke 22:32

Prayer is talking with God and telling Him you love Him, conversing with God about all the things that are important in life, both large and small, and being assured that He is listening.

—C. Neil Strait

YEA, MANY PEOPLE AND STRONG NATIONS SHALL COME TO SEEK THE LORD OF HOSTS IN JERUSALEM, AND TO PRAY BEFORE THE LORD.

—Zechariah 8:22 KJV

_____
_____
_____
_____
_____
_____
_____
_____
_____
_____
_____
_____
_____
_____
_____
_____
_____
_____
_____
_____
_____
_____
_____
_____
_____
_____
_____
_____
_____

AND WHEN HE HAD SENT THE MULTITUDES AWAY, HE WENT UP INTO
A MOUNTAIN APART TO PRAY: AND WHEN THE EVENING WAS COME,
HE WAS THERE ALONE.

—Matthew 14:23 KJV

Prayer opens the heart to God, and it is the means by which the soul, though empty, is filled by God.

—*John Bunyan*

BUT WHEN YOU ARE PRAYING, FIRST FORGIVE ANYONE YOU ARE
HOLDING A GRUDGE AGAINST, SO THAT YOUR FATHER IN HEAVEN
WILL FORGIVE YOUR SINS, TOO.

—*Mark 11:25 NLT*

When a Christian shuns fellowship with other Christians, the devil smiles. When he stops studying the Bible, the devil laughs. When he stops praying, the devil shouts for joy.

—*Corrie ten Boom*

BLESS THOSE WHO CURSE YOU, AND PRAY FOR THOSE
WHO SPITEFULLY USE YOU.

—Luke 6:28

All this trying leads up to the vital moment at which you turn to God and say, "You must do this. I can't."

—*C. S. Lewis*

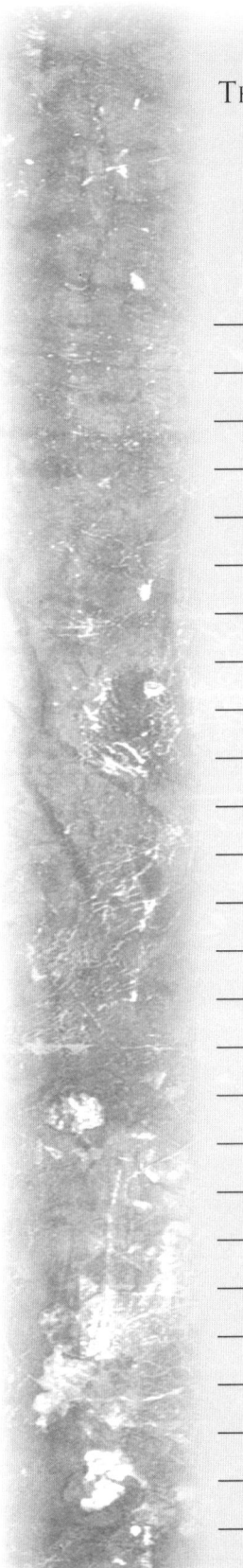

THEREFORE SAID HE UNTO THEM, THE HARVEST TRULY IS GREAT, BUT THE LABOURERS ARE FEW: PRAY YE THEREFORE THE LORD OF THE HARVEST, THAT HE WOULD SEND FORTH LABOURERS INTO HIS HARVEST.

—Luke 10:2 KJV

Let this be thy whole endeavor, this thy prayer, this thy desire, —that thou mayest be stripped of all selfishness, and with entire simplicity follow Jesus only.

—*Thomas à Kempis*

TREAT MY PRAYER AS SWEET INCENSE RISING; MY RAISED HANDS ARE
MY EVENING PRAYERS.

—*Psalm 141:2 THE MESSAGE*

We must move from asking God to take care of the things that are breaking our hearts, to praying about the things that are breaking His heart.

—*Margaret Gibb*

LET MY PRAYER COME BEFORE THEE: INCLINE THINE EAR
UNTO MY CRY.

—*Psalm 88:2 KJV*

Pray often, for prayer is a shield to the soul, a sacrifice to God and a scourge for Satan.
—John Bunyan

THEN JESUS TOLD HIS DISCIPLES A PARABLE TO SHOW THEM THAT
THEY SHOULD ALWAYS PRAY AND NOT GIVE UP.

—Luke 18:1 NIV

Nothing can keep you from being directly connected to God if you want to be.

— *Thelma Wells*

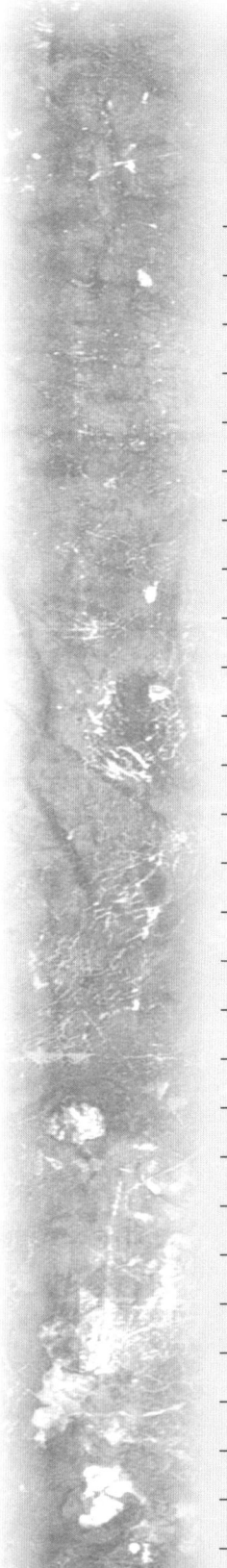

"WHY ARE YOU SLEEPING?" HE ASKED. "GET UP AND PRAY.
OTHERWISE TEMPTATION WILL OVERPOWER YOU."

— Luke 22:46 NLT

Don't stop praying even if you've been doing it for a long time and it seems as if God must not be listening.

—*Stormie Omartian*

I PRAY FOR THEM. I DO NOT PRAY FOR THE WORLD BUT FOR THOSE WHOM YOU HAVE GIVEN ME, FOR THEY ARE YOURS.

—John 17:9

Pray, and let God worry.
—Martin Luther

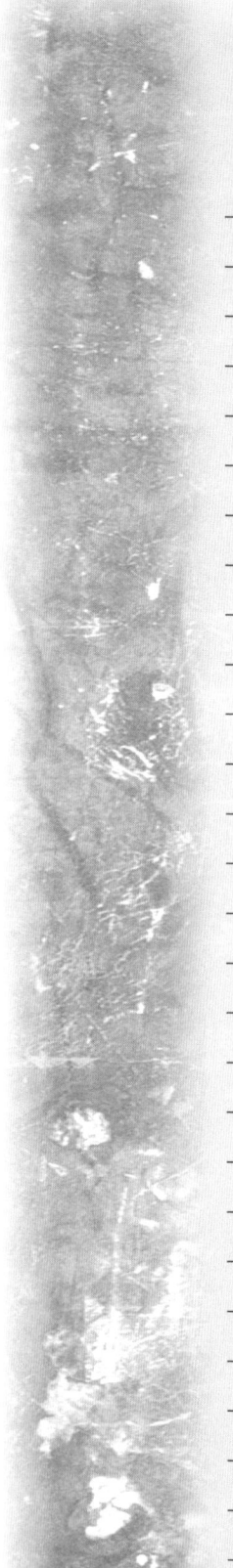

CONTINUE IN PRAYER, AND WATCH IN THE SAME
WITH THANKSGIVING.

—Colossians 4:2 KJV

I have had prayers answered—most strangely sometimes—but I think our heavenly Father's loving kindness has been even more evident in what He has refused me.

—*Lewis Carroll*

PRAY WITHOUT CEASING.

—*1 Thessalonians 5:17*

Prayer is an ordinance of God, that must continue with a soul so long as it is on this side glory.

—*John Bunyan*

First of all, then, I urge that supplications, prayers, intercessions, and thanksgivings be made for all men, for kings and all who are in high positions, that we may lead a quiet and peaceable life, godly and respectful in every way.

—1 Timothy 2:1-2 NRSV

God's hearing of our prayers doth not depend upon sanctification, but upon Christ's intercession; not upon what we are in ourselves, but what we are in the Lord Jesus; both our persons and our prayers are acceptable in the beloved.

— Thomas Brooks

REPENT OF THIS WICKEDNESS AND PRAY TO THE LORD. PERHAPS HE
WILL FORGIVE YOU FOR HAVING SUCH A THOUGHT IN YOUR HEART.

—*Acts 8:22 NIV*

A simple grateful thought turned heavenwards

is the most perfect prayer.

—Gotthold Lessing

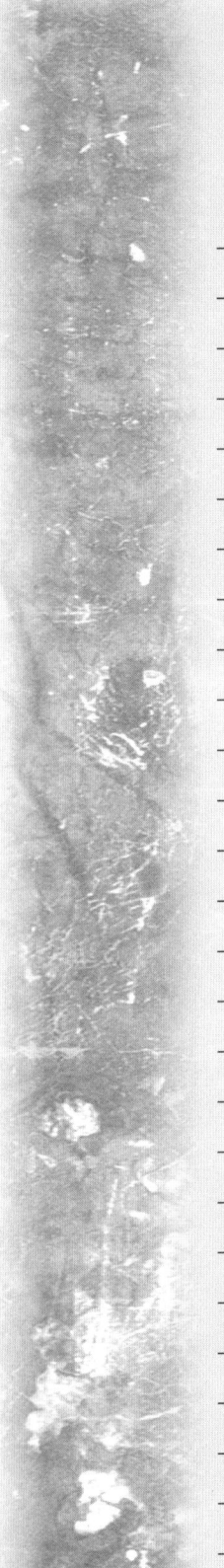

BUT AS FOR ME, MY PRAYER IS UNTO THEE, O LORD, IN AN
ACCEPTABLE TIME: O GOD, IN THE MULTITUDE OF THY MERCY
HEAR ME, IN THE TRUTH OF THY SALVATION.

—Psalm 69:13 KJV

Keep praying, but be thankful that God's answers are wiser
than your prayers.
—William Culbertson

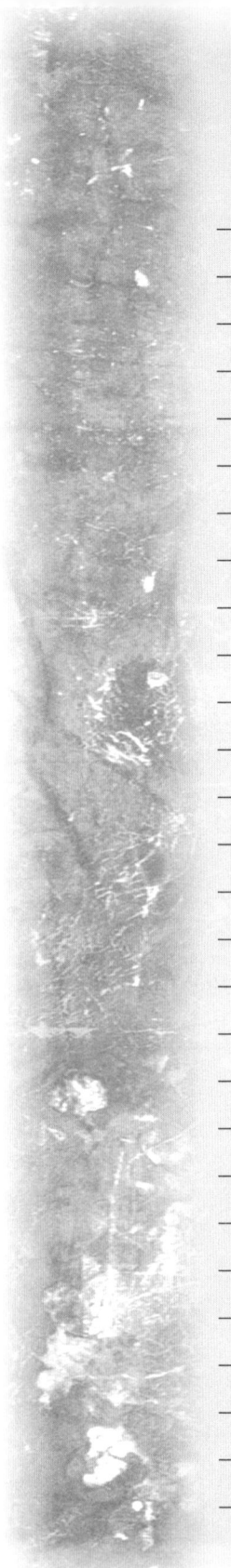

WATCH AND PRAY, LEST YOU ENTER INTO TEMPTATION. THE SPIRIT INDEED IS WILLING, BUT THE FLESH IS WEAK.

—*Matthew 26:41*

Prayer is nothing but the breathing that out before the Lord, that was first breathed into us by the Spirit of the Lord.

— Thomas Brooks

I WANT MEN EVERYWHERE TO LIFT UP HOLY HANDS IN PRAYER,
WITHOUT ANGER OR DISPUTING.

—1 Timothy 2:8 NIV

Prayer is as natural an expression of faith as breathing is of life.
—Jonathan Edwards

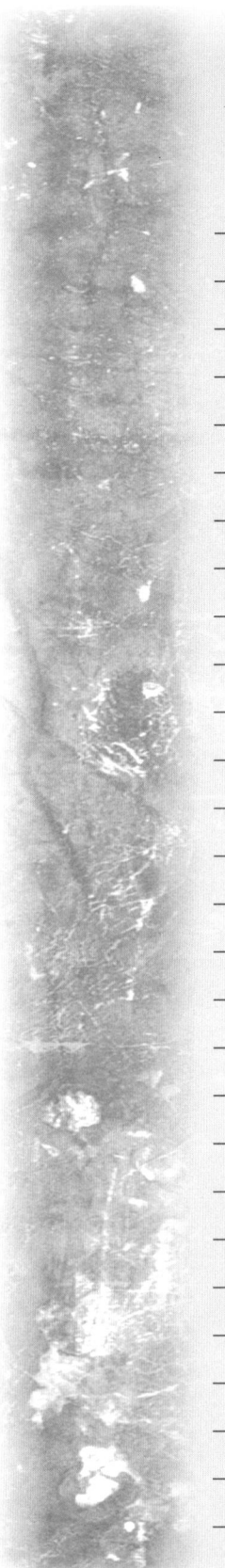

ANYONE WHO IS HAVING TROUBLES SHOULD PRAY. ANYONE WHO IS HAPPY SHOULD SING PRAISES.

—*James 5:13 NCV*

Prayer is our path to the adventure of building a relationship with our Savior.
—Christa Kinde

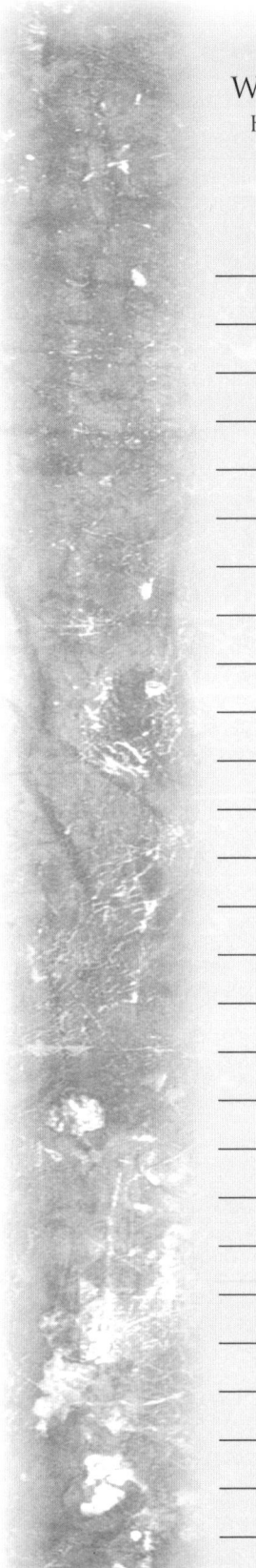

WE DO NOT KNOW HOW TO PRAY AS WE SHOULD. BUT THE SPIRIT HIMSELF SPEAKS TO GOD FOR US, EVEN BEGS GOD FOR US WITH DEEP FEELINGS THAT WORDS CANNOT EXPLAIN.

—*Romans 8:28 NCV*

Prayer has mighty power to move mountains because the Holy Spirit is ready both to encourage our praying and to remove the mountains hindering us. Prayer has the power to change mountains into highways.

—Wesley L. Duewel

BUT WE WILL GIVE OURSELVES CONTINUALLY TO PRAYER, AND TO THE MINISTRY OF THE WORD.

—Acts 6:4 KJV

The best and sweetest flowers of Paradise God gives to his people when they are upon their knees. Prayer is the gate of heaven, a key to let us in to Paradise.

— Thomas Brooks

PRAY FIRST THAT THE LORD'S MESSAGE WILL SPREAD RAPIDLY AND BE HONORED WHEREVER IT GOES, JUST AS WHEN IT CAME TO YOU.

—2 Thessalonians 3:1

Ask God's blessing on your work, but don't ask him

to do it for you.

—Dame Flora Robson

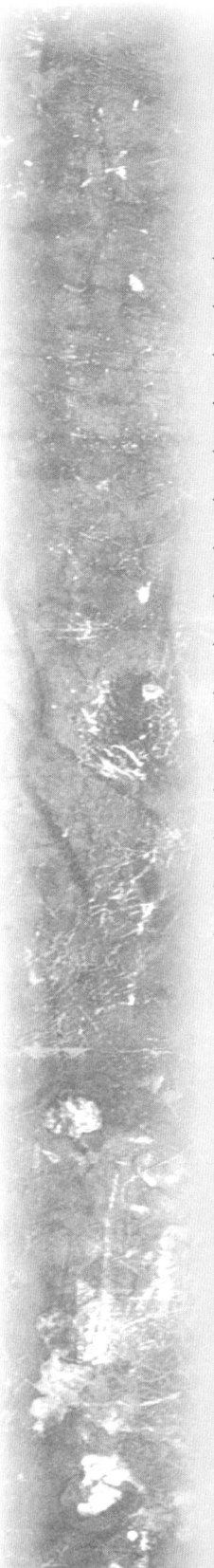

PRAY FOR US; FOR WE ARE CONFIDENT THAT WE HAVE A GOOD
CONSCIENCE, IN ALL THINGS DESIRING TO LIVE HONORABLY.

—Hebrews 13:18

There are some favors the Almighty does not grant either the first, or the second, or the third time you ask him, because he wishes you to pray for a long time and often. He wills this delay to keep you in a state of humility and self-contempt and make you realize the value of his graces.

—John Eudes

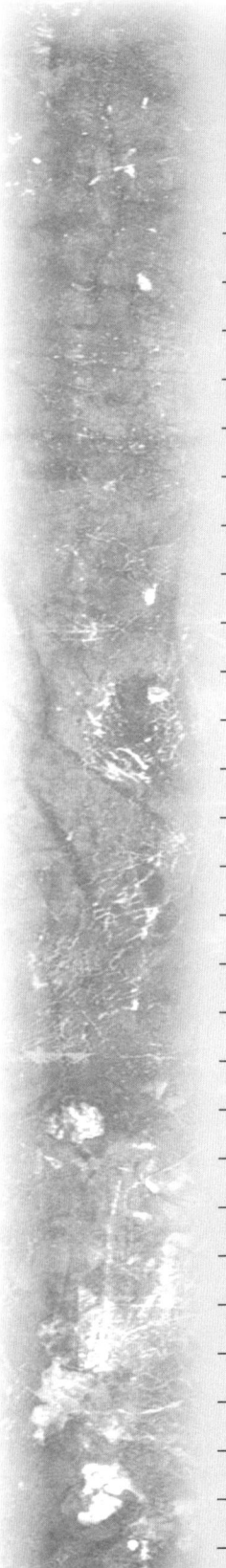

AND THE PRAYER OF FAITH WILL SAVE THE SICK, AND THE LORD
WILL RAISE HIM UP.

—James 5:15

Those blessings are sweetest that are won with prayers and worn with thanks.

— Thomas Goodwin

The quiet hour of prayer is one of the most favorable opportunities He has in which to speak to us seriously. In quietude and solitude before the face of God, our souls can hear better than at any other time.

—*O. Hallesby*

ACKNOWLEDGMENTS

Grateful acknowledgment is made to the following for permission to reprint copyrighted material:

Adventurous Prayer © 2003, excerpted by permission of Thomas Nelson Publishers.

Checklist for Life © 2002 GRQ, Inc., excerpted by permission of Thomas Nelson Publishers.

Donelson Fellowship, The ©2004, *Pocket Papers, http://www.donelson.org/pocket.cfm.*

Franklin Graham, excerpted by permission of Thomas Nelson Publishers from the book entitled *All for Jesus* ©2003 Franklin Graham with Ross Rhoads.

Cynthia Heald, excerpted by permission of Thomas Nelson Publishers from the book entitled *Becoming a Woman of Faith* © 2000.

—*Becoming a Woman of Grace* © 1998, excerpted by permission of Thomas Nelson Publishers.

Barbara Johnson, excerpted by permission of W Publishing Group, a division of Thomas Nelson Publishers from the book entitled *The Great Adventure* © 2002.

—*Devotions for a Sensational Life* © 2002, excerpted by permission of Thomas Nelson Publishers.

—*Daily Splashes of Joy* © 2000, excerpted by permission of W Publishing Group, a division of Thomas Nelson Publishers.

—*Irrepressible Hope*, © 2003, excerpted by permission of W Publishing Group, a division of Thomas Nelson Publishers © 2003.

Nicole Johnson, excerpted by permission of W Publishing Group, a division of Thomas Nelson Publishers from the book entitled *Irrepressible Hope* © 2002.

Anne Graham Lotz, excerpted by permission of W Publishing Group, a division of Thomas Nelson Publishers from the book entitled *Just Give Me Jesus* © 2003 by Anne Graham Lotz.

Max Lucado, excerpted by permission of J. Countryman, a division of Thomas Nelson Publishers from the book entitled *Grace for the Moment* © 2002.

—*In the Grip of Grace* © 1996 by Max Lucado, excerpted by permission of W Publishing Group, a division of Thomas Nelson Publishers.

—*A Gentle Thunder* © 1995, by Max Lucado, excerpted by permission of W Publishing Group, a division of Thomas Nelson Publishers.

Catherine Marshall, excerpted by permission of J. Countryman, a division of Thomas Nelson Publishers from the book entitled *Moments That Matter* © 2001 by Marshall-LeSourd LLC.

John C. Maxwell, excerpted by permission of J. Countryman, a division of Thomas Nelson Publishers from the book entitled *Leadership* © 2001 by John C. Maxwell.

Robert J. Morgan, excerpted by permission of Thomas Nelson Publishers from the book entitled *Real Stories for the Soul* © 2000 by Robert J. Morgan.

—*Nelson's Annual Preacher's Sourcebook* © 2004 by Robert J. Morgan, by permission of Thomas Nelson Publishers.